# I AM AUTISTIC
## And I Can Be Anything!

Written By:
Brad Trice &
Domonique Trice

Illustrated By:
Kendrick Murray

This book belongs to:

_____

4

**Dedicated to:**

BJ and Britton and all of the
families living on the Spectrum.

Hello World!
My name is B.J.
I am Autistic and
I can be ANYTHING!

I can be a pro **ATHLETE**, leading my team to victory!

Or I can be an
**ENTREPRENUER**
and create a billion
dollar company!

I can be a **MUSICIAN** and create sounds that make you move.

I can be a best-selling **AUTHOR** of books for any mood.

I can be a great **ACTIVIST** that does all sorts of good!

I can be an **INVENTOR** and make things I never thought I could.

I can be a **SCIENTIST** and create a winning solution,

Or be an **ENGINEER** and solve problems like pollution!

I can be a **LAWYER** and work my way up to the West Wing.

# I may learn and do things differently, but

# I CAN BE
# ANYTHING!!!